SUNSPOT

Written by Matt Weber
Illustrated by Erin Reilly

RPSS - Rock Paper Safety Scissors Publishing
Buffalo, New York

Copyright © 2023 by Matt Weber
All rights reserved. No part of this publication may be reproduced, distributed, or transmitted in any form or by any means, including photocopying, recording, or other electronic or mechanical methods, without the prior written permission of the publisher, except in the case of brief quotations embodied in critical reviews and certain other non-commercial uses permitted by copyright law.

RPSS - Rock, Paper, Safety Scissors Publishing,
429 Englewood Avenue, Kenmore, NY 14223
publisher@rockpapersafetyscissors.com

ISBN-13: 978-1-956688-14-6

Sunspot - Hardcover

19 20 21 22 23   6 5 4 3 2 1

--

First Printing: 2023
--
Printed in the USA

RPSS - Rock Paper Safety Scissors Publishing
Buffalo, New York

To Autumn,
in a father's life of half finished ideas,
you were the reason to see this through.

Love, Dad

Sunspot the whale shark swims through the ocean. There's rarely a moment she isn't in motion.

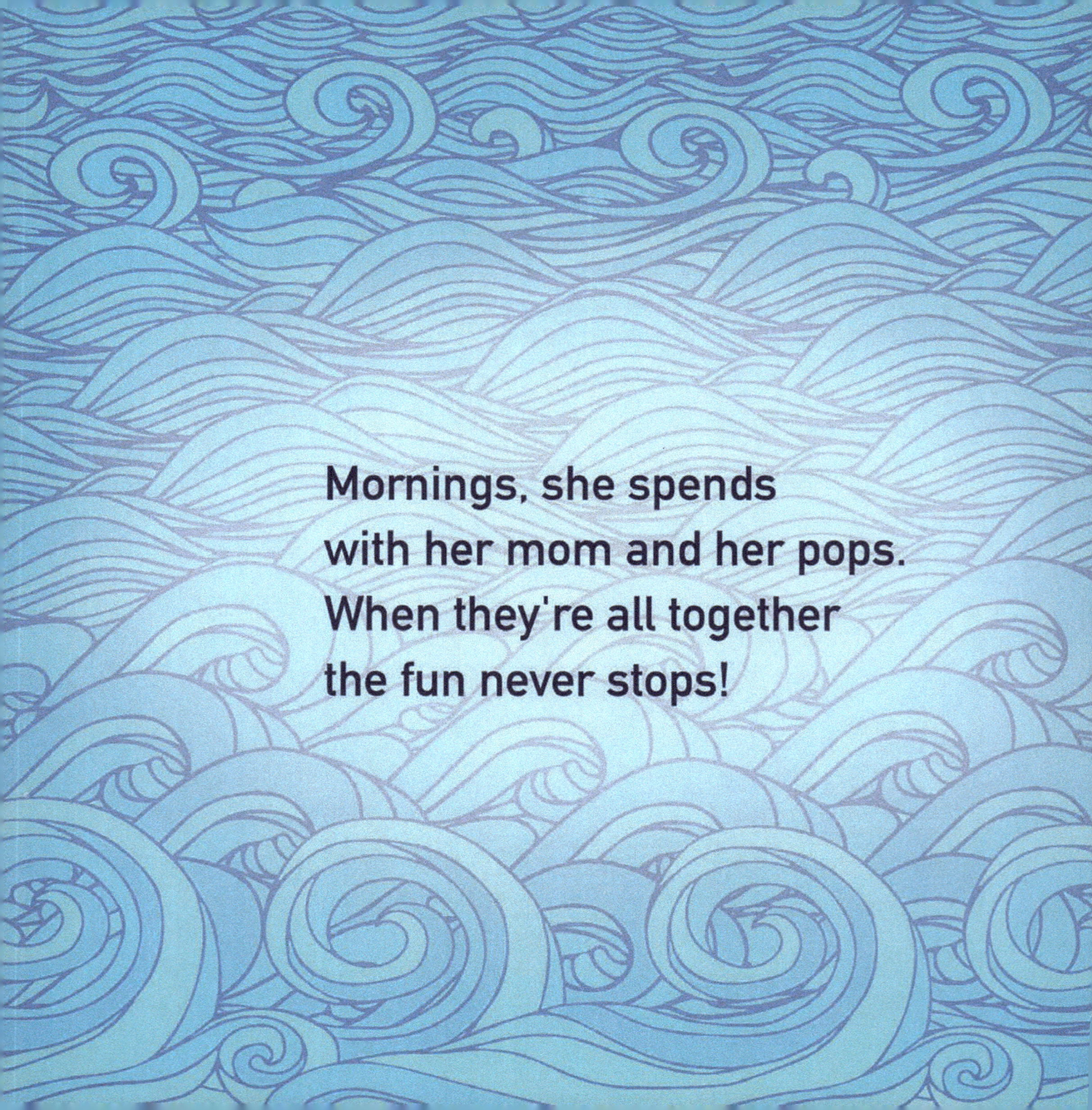

Mornings, she spends
with her mom and her pops.
When they're all together
the fun never stops!

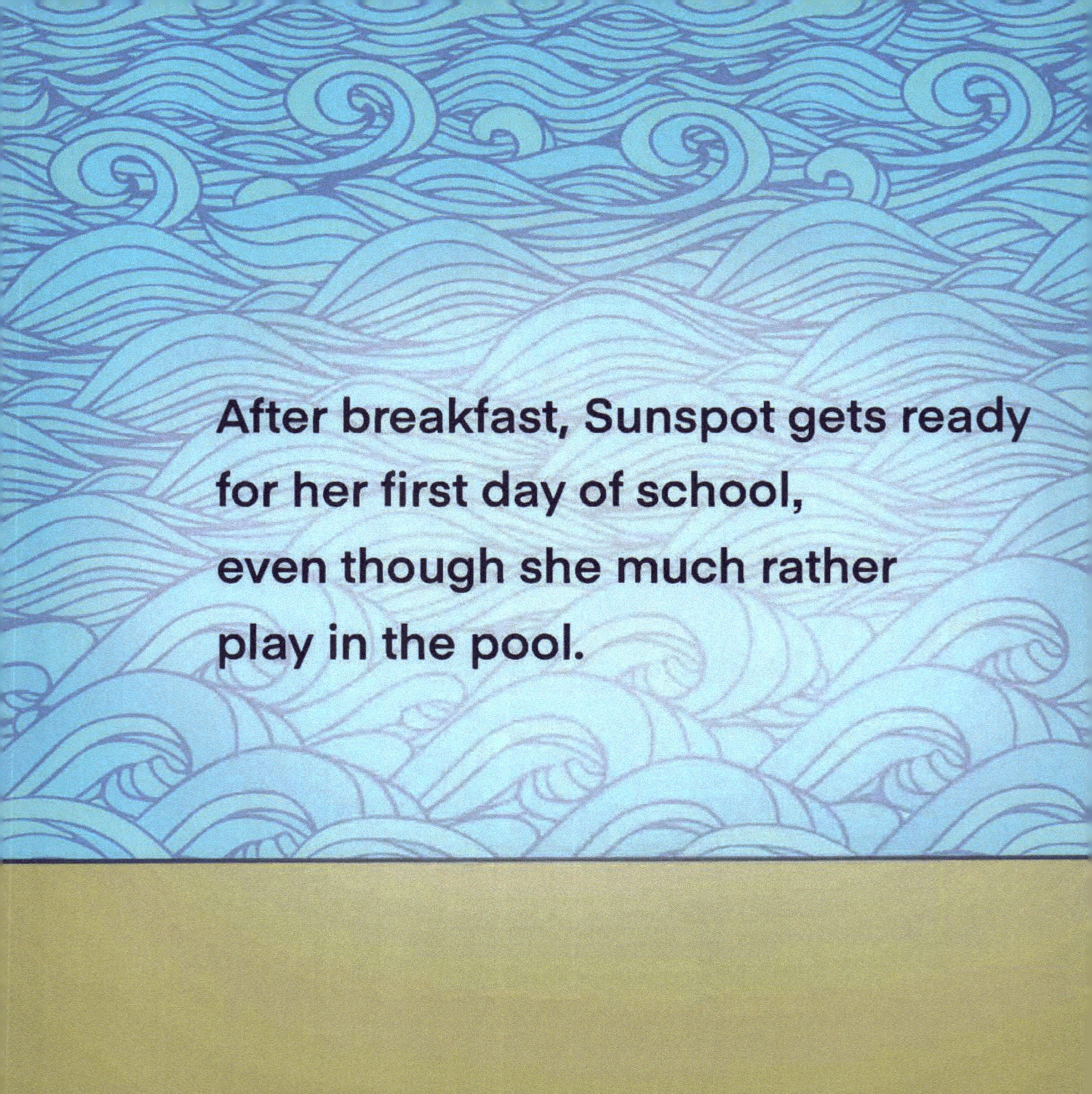

After breakfast, Sunspot gets ready
for her first day of school,
even though she much rather
play in the pool.

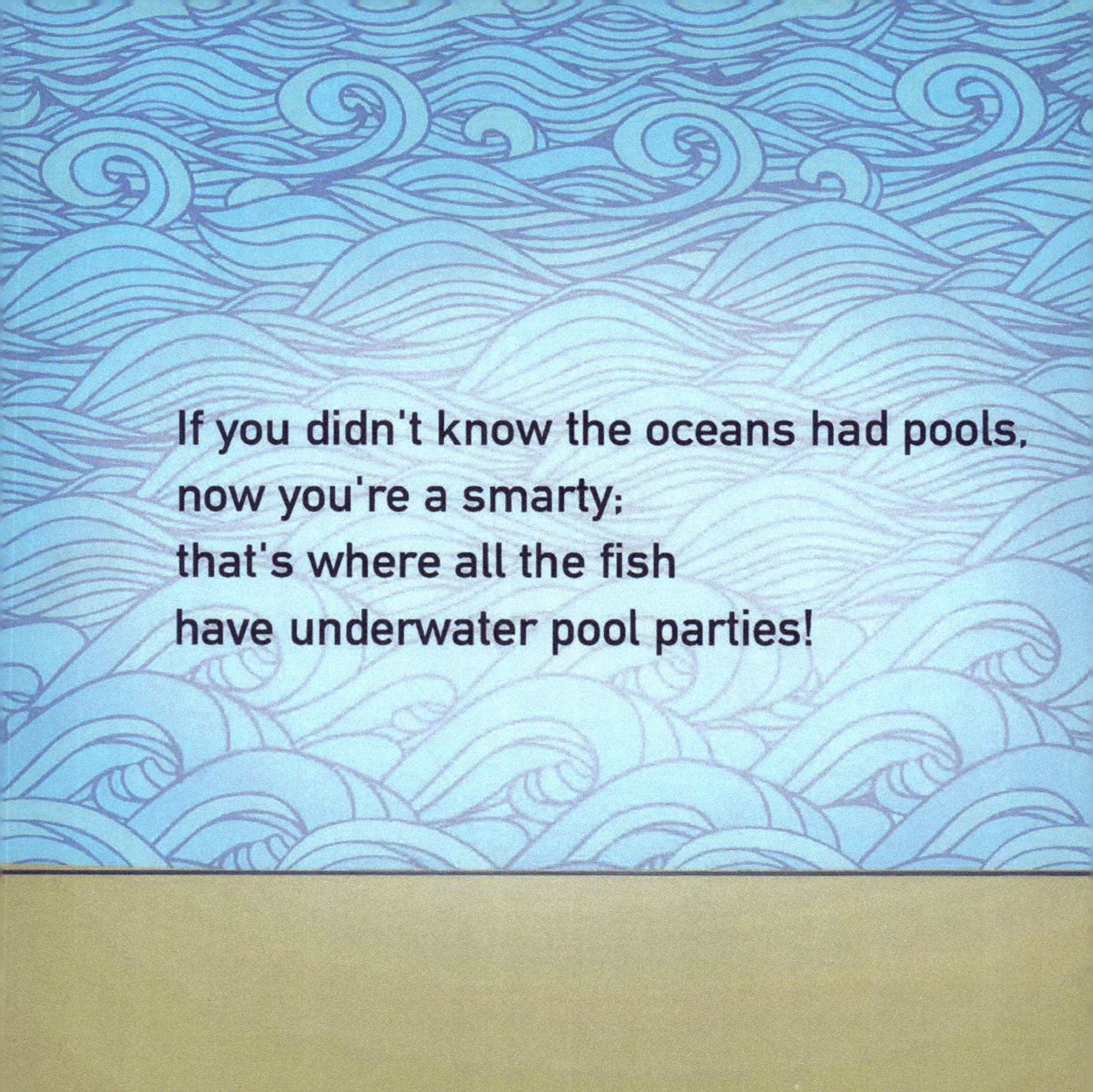

If you didn't know the oceans had pools,
now you're a smarty;
that's where all the fish
have underwater pool parties!

When she arrives at her class,
lo and behold,
she sees a room full of whale shark
calves from a different mold.

Other kids in the class
had spots all around,
and when Sunspot noticed
she immediately frowned.

She never once ever had to consider
that the way she
and other whale sharks look
would differ.

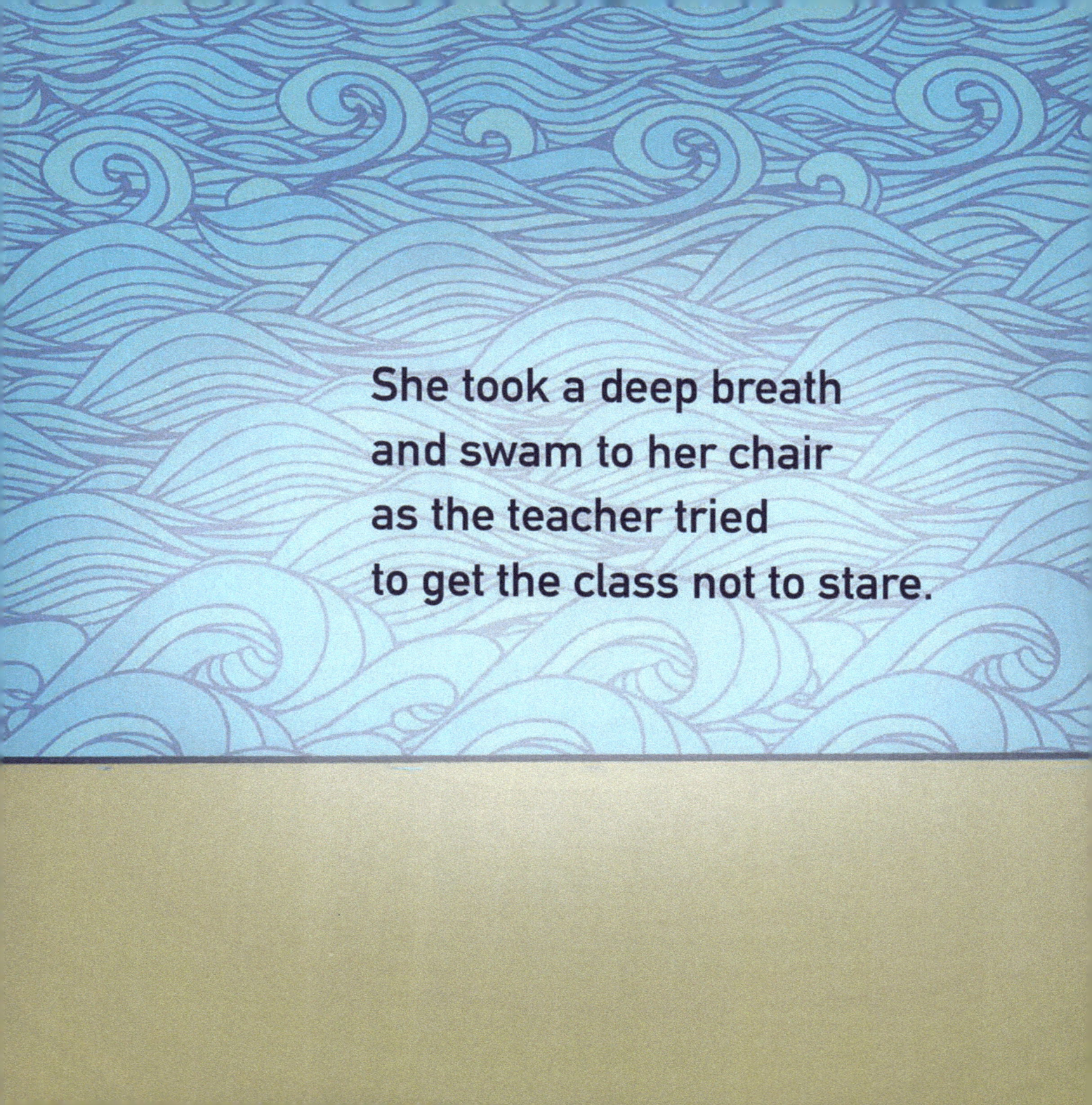

She took a deep breath
and swam to her chair
as the teacher tried
to get the class not to stare.

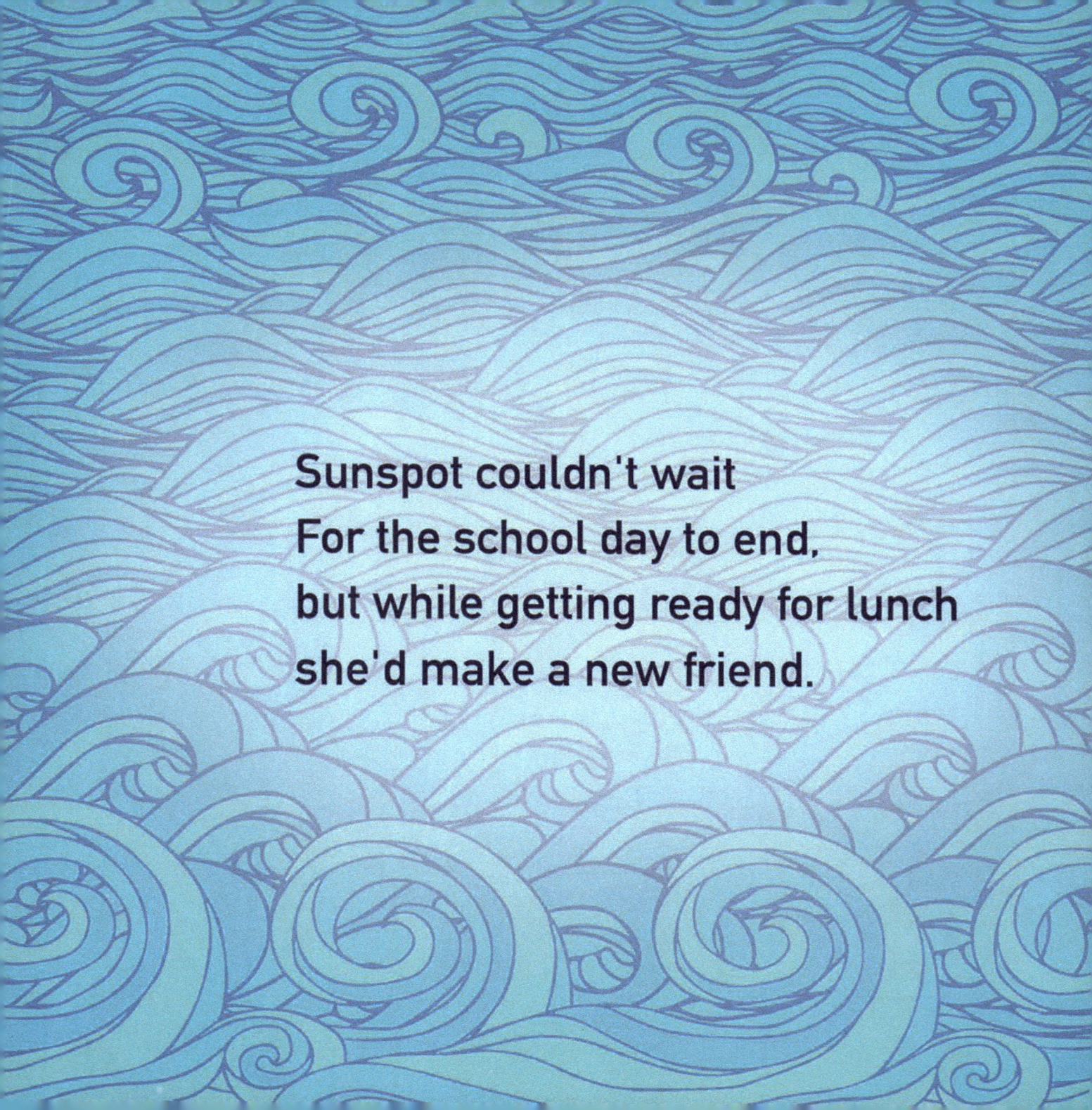

Sunspot couldn't wait
For the school day to end,
but while getting ready for lunch
she'd make a new friend.

Glide swam up to Sunspot with glee,
and when he approached
only one spot she could see.

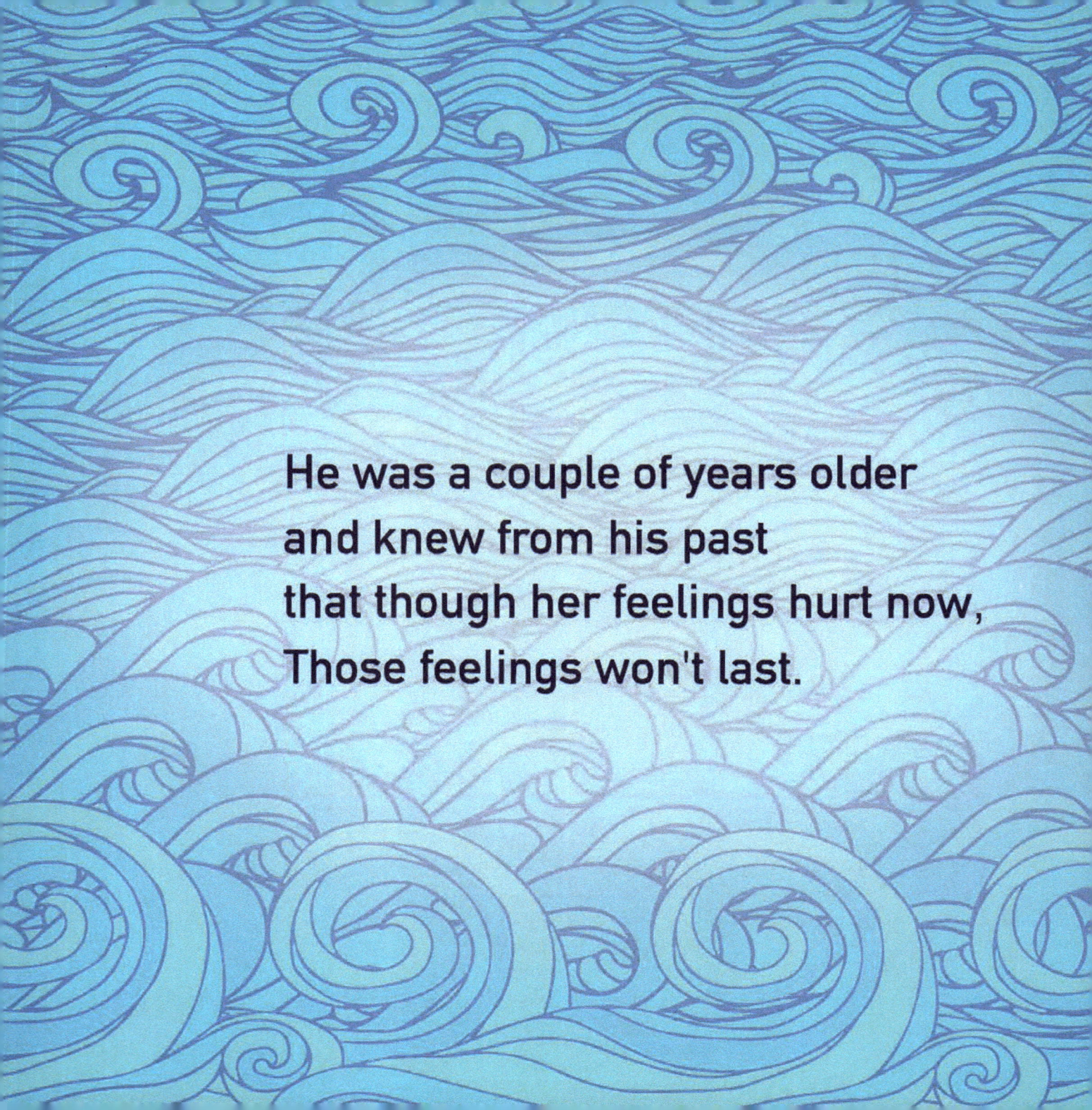

He was a couple of years older
and knew from his past
that though her feelings hurt now,
Those feelings won't last.

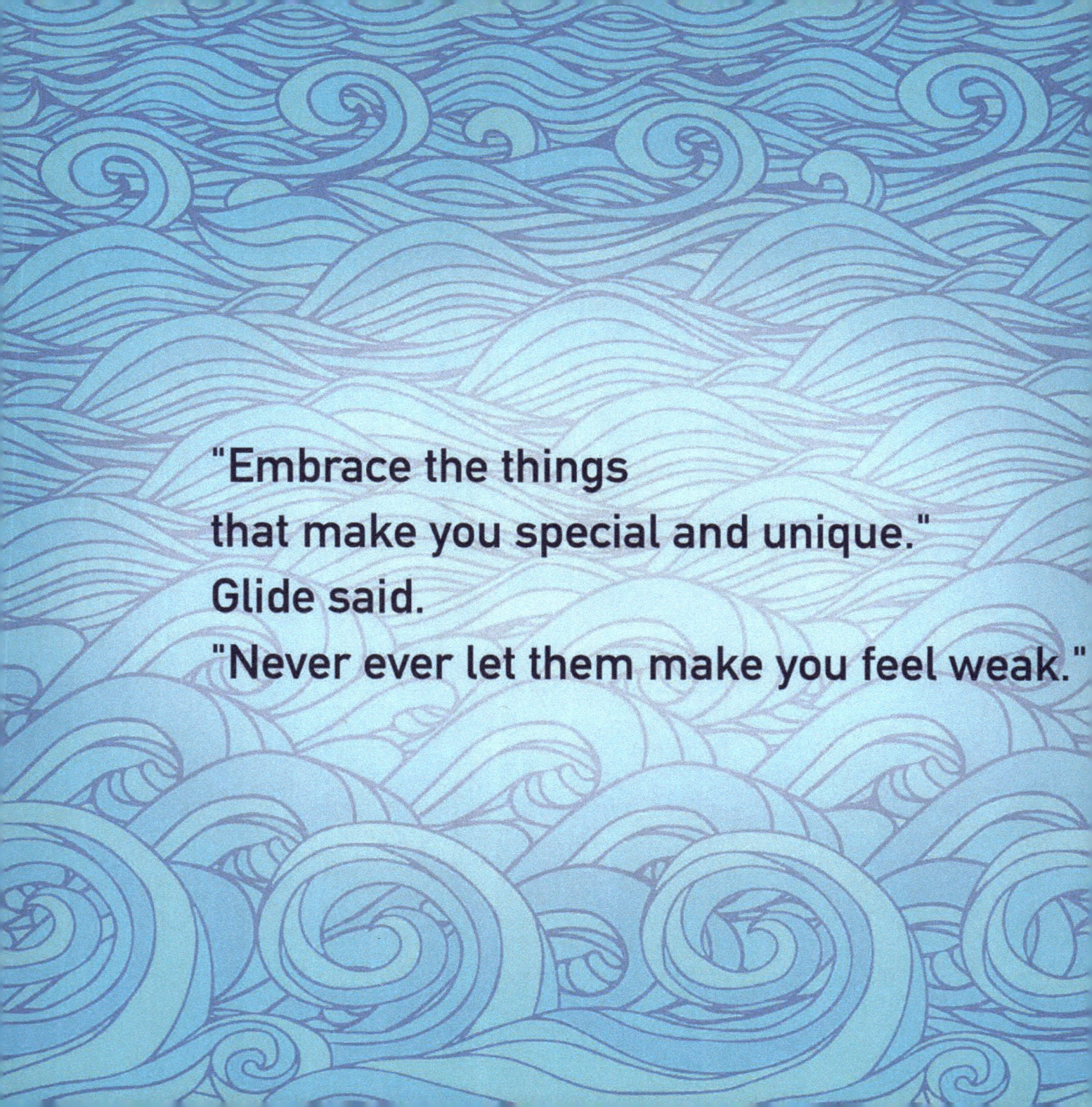

"Embrace the things
that make you special and unique."
Glide said.
"Never ever let them make you feel weak."

His words led Sunspot
to a gill-to-gill smile,
one that she would carry
for quite a while.

When Sunspot got home,
she told mom and dad about her day.
Forgetting the morning,
she had only great things to say!

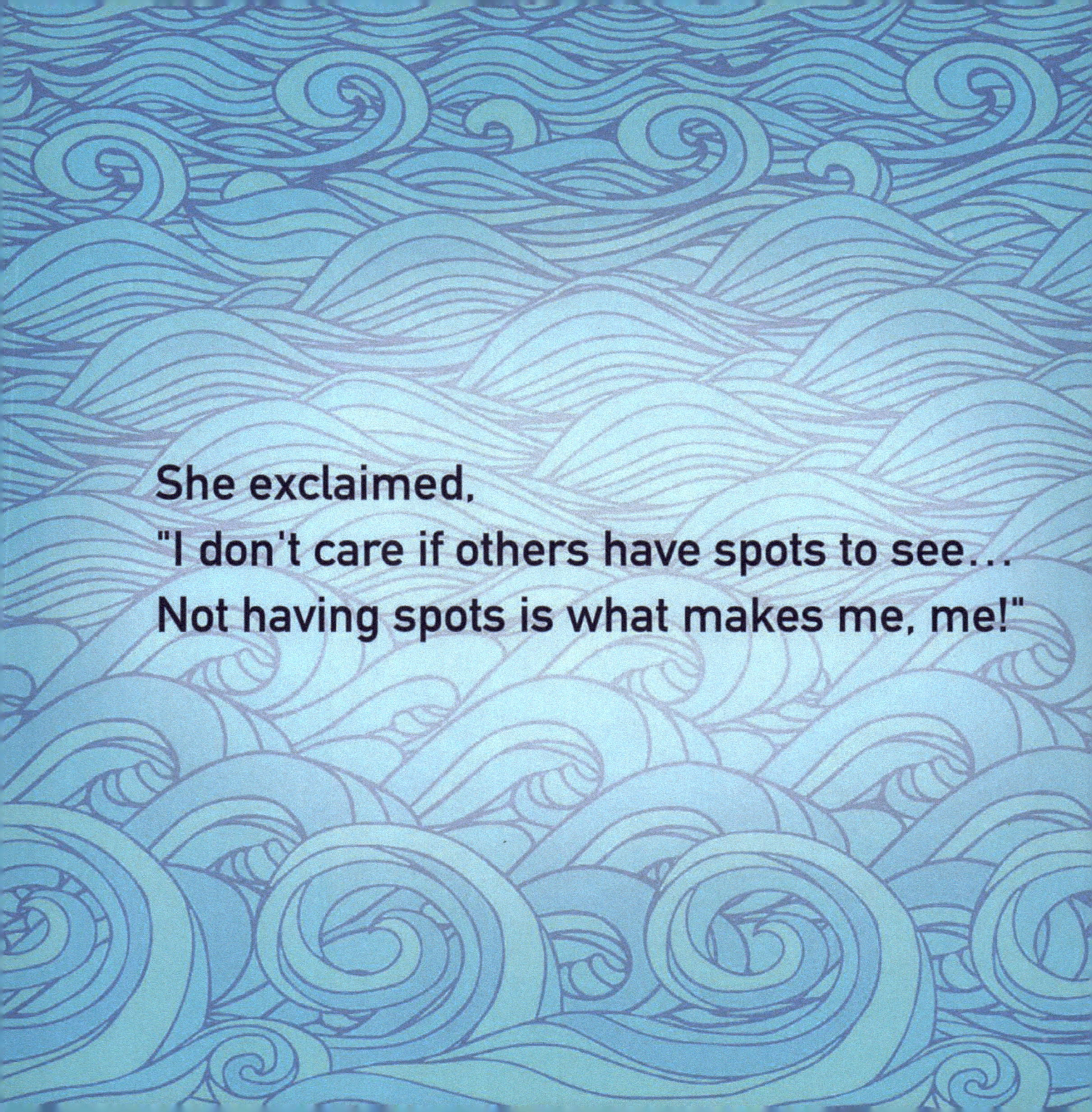

She exclaimed,
"I don't care if others have spots to see...
Not having spots is what makes me, me!"

The End

CPSIA information can be obtained
at www.ICGtesting.com
Printed in the USA
LVHW010009080623
749069LV00016B/8